A MOTHER & DAUGHTER
MEMOIRS OF
LOVE, DESIRE, PAIN & INSPIRATION

BY: **ROBIN T. DORSEY & RENITA T. MOCK**

If you purchase this book without a cover you should be aware that this book may have been stolen property and reported as "unsold and destroyed" to the publisher. In such case neither the author nor the publisher has received any payment for this "stripped book."

This is a poetry book that represents a compilation of poems of "Love, Desire, Pain, & Inspiration" from the views of "a mother and daughter duo Robin T. Dorsey & Renita T. Mock". Some poems were written for various individuals and some in the eyes of other people from our perspective.

DORSEY PUBLISHING, LLC
"Let's Make Your Dreams A Reality"

Fort Washington, MD
www.DorseyPublishing.com

A MOTHER AND DAUGHER MEMOIRS OF
LOVE, DESIRE, PAIN & INSPIRATION

Copyright © 2014 by Robin T. Dorsey & Renita T. Mock

All rights reserved, including the right to reproduce this book or portions thereof in any form whatsoever.

ISBN (13)   978-0-615-94473-9

ISBN (10)   0615944736

Library of Congress Control Number (LCCN) 2014932659

Manufactured in the United States of America

Cover Photo By: Linda Day
Creative Design: HotBookCovers.com
Illustrations By: Briana Smith

DEDICATION

The Legacy of Renita T. Mock

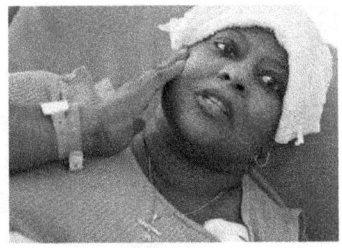

This book is dedicated to the late Renita T. Mock. Ms. Mock was an amazing woman. She lived a good life and fought a good fight. She is the Co-Author of this book. Ms. Mock was a healer, an inspiration to everyone she came in contact with and a blessing. She always gave her last to help take care of others. She had a heart of gold and the spirit of an angel. Ms. Mock died on March 12, 2013 of Breast Cancer. She was loved by many and is truly missed.

The Fantastic Four

The Fantastic Four consist of Renita T. Mock whom is the mother of her three extraordinary children; Denitria S. Washington, Robin T. Dorsey, and Lakisha M. Mock. Through thick and thin they have always stayed together until the end. These remarkable women are a force to be reckoned with.

THIS BOOK IS A TRIBUTE TO
"THE FANTASTIC FOUR"

ACKNOWLEDGEMENTS

We would like to thank our family, and friends who stood by us through the loss of our mother. We would also like to acknowledge Hot Book Covers (HBC) **www.hotbookcovers.com** for our astonishing book cover, and Briana Smith for the remarkable inside book illustrations.

A special thanks goes to the honorable and remarkable Renita T. Mock for giving us life, and love. Your legacy lives on through "The Fantastic Four".

Follow Us on Twitter:
@Dorseypublish
@Robintdorsey

Follow Us on Facebook:
https://www.facebook.com/dorseypublishing

Visit our Websites:

http://www.dorseypublishing.com

http://www.robindorsey.com

A MOTHER & DAUGHTER
MEMOIRS OF
LOVE, DESIRE, PAIN & INSPIRATION

CONTENTS

1	**Chapter: Love**	**1**
	Loving You *(RTD)*	3
	Little Special Bee *(RTD)*	4
	You Showed me Love *(RTD)*	5
	I Chose to be with You *(RTD)*	6-7
	A Mother's Love *(RTM)*	8
	Arrow of Explosion *(RTM)*	9
	Love Unconditionally *(RTM)*	10
	Me & My Girls *(RTM)*	11
	In the Right Side of my Heart *(RTM)*	12
	My Friends & Me *(RTM)*	13
	The Beat of My Heart *(RTM)*	14
	My Dream *(RTM)*	15
	The Little People *(RTM)*	16
	My Full Size Luxury *(RTM)*	17
	My Precious Stones *(RTM)*	18
	On this Day I Pledge *(RTM)*	20-21
	The Day I Married *(RTM)*	22
	We Are Connected *(RTM)*	23
	Wedding *(RTM)*	24
	Illustration by Briana Smith	26
2	**Chapter: Desire**	**27**
	The Passion Between Us *(RTD)*	28
	Can I Have Some of That *(RTD)*	29
	A Long Ride Home *(RTD)*	30-31
	Home Alone *(RTD)*	32-33
	Riding With My Mystery Man *(RTD)*	34-36
	You Unleashed the Freak *(RTD)*	38
	You Make Me Feel Like *(RTD)*	39
	Oh Yes *(RTD)*	40
	Why All of Me *(RTM)*	41
	Sex *(RTM)*	42
	Illustration by Briana Smith	44

3	**Chapter: Pain**	**45**
	Day Dreamer *(RTD)*	46
	Despite Of *(RTD)*	47
	Can you Handle It *(RTD)*	48-49
	Can I Wait to See *(RTD)*	50-51
	Don't Try to Control Me *(RTD)*	52
	People will Let You Down *(RTD)*	53
	That's That Bullsh*t *(RTD)*	54-55
	Time to Walk Away *(RTD)*	56
	You Said You Had My Back *(RTD)*	57
	You are a Liar *(RTD)*	58
	Why are you so Selfish *(RTD)*	59
	You Thought I Would Fail *(RTD)*	60
	I Thought You Loved Me *(RTD)*	61
	In Care of My Child *(RTM)*	62
	The Life of an Officer *(RTM)*	63
	It Just Doesn't Matter *(RTM)*	64
	In Time *(RTM)*	66-67
	The Midnight Hour *(RTM)*	68
	The Pain of Love *(RTM)*	69
	Winter Months *(RTM)*	70
	Wondering What *(RTM)*	71
	Illustration by Briana Smith	72
4	**Chapter: Inspiration**	**73**
	A Path *(RTD)*	74
	Always There *(RTD)*	75
	Do You Believe *(RTD)*	76
	If I Don't Make It Past Tomorrow *(RTD)*	77
	Friends *(RTD)*	78
	The Day you were Born *(RTD)*	79
	I Strive *(RTD)*	80
	Dreams Do Come True *(RTD)*	81
	My Goals *(RTD)*	82
	I was Broken *(RTD)*	83
	Living Life & Loving It *(RTD)*	84-85
	Procrastination (RTD)	86
	God Chose Me *(RTD)*	87
	A Day of Thanksgiving *(RTM)*	88
	Flowers *(RTM)*	89
	God Almighty *(RTM)*	90
	Happiness *(RTM)*	91
	Heaven Help Us *(RTM)*	92

I'm Free *(RTM)*	93
It's Up to You *(RTM)*	94-95
Living *(RTM)*	96
Time Is Near *(RTM)*	97
When I Go Home *(RTM)*	98
You Can't Stop *(RTM)*	99
If I Could It Over *(RTM)*	100
About the Authors	103

A Mother & Daughter Memoirs of Love, Desire, Pain & Inspiration

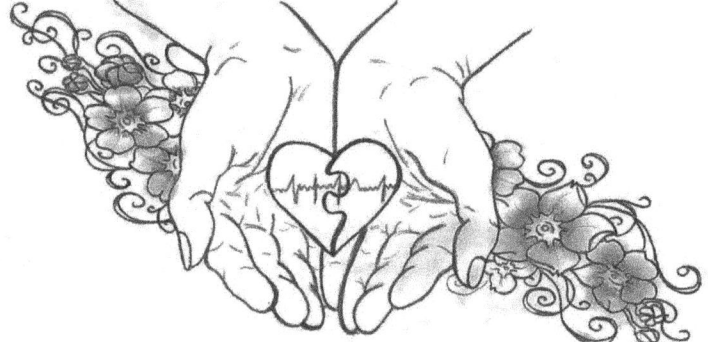

1

Love

*"Love is tender, Love is kind,
Love sends tingles up your spine"*

By: Robin T. Dorsey

A Mother & Daughter Memoirs of Love, Desire, Pain & Inspiration

"Loving You"

I wanted to love you,
The first day I met you,
My heart just wouldn't let it be true,
So, I didn't realize how much I needed you,
Loved you, or wanted you,
Always wondering could it be true,
To love you!

Now you're gone,
And we have a past,
Because I didn't try to make it last,

Always wanting to be with one another,
With a single call we found each other,
Now, at last we can have a blast,
A second chance is what we have at last,

Loving you isn't hard to do,
Loving you is all I want to do,
Through all the doubt we can make it true,

"Now, the choice is all up to you"

A Mother & Daughter Memoirs of Love, Desire, Pain & Inspiration

"Little Special Bee"

I'm glad you came into my life…

Since the day you came into my life,
You have brought me joy!

You showed me how to Love,
How to give Love,
And how to be Loved!

Now, with the Love,
You gave to me to,
I give to thee,

Loving you,
Who would have ever thought it to be?
So, easily to Love thee,
You're my little special bee,
And there's no one else for me,

Loving me,
Loving thee,
Forever & ever is all it can be,
I promise never to leave,
My little special bee!

I'm glad you came into my life,
Now, I really want you to know,

"Are you ready for me to be your Wife?"

"You Showed Me Love"

You showed me love by…the look in your eyes,
You showed me love by…your assertiveness and attentiveness,
You showed me love by…your kind and tender words,
You showed me love by…lending a listening ear,
You showed me love by…inspiring me to be all that I can be,
You showed me love by…showing me how to let my hair down,
Have fun, and live in the moment,
You showed me love by…your nice warm embracing hugs,
You showed me love by…always putting a smile on my face,
You showed me love by…your gentle and tender caresses,
You showed me love by…your sensual kisses,
You showed me love by…your erotic massages,
You showed me love by…your vivacious tongue lashes,
You showed me love by…your deep penetrations,
You showed me love by…your cuddling sensations!

"Because you showed me love…Now I know how to give unconditional love back, too"

"I Chose To Be With You"

I chose to be with you because of your smiling face,
I chose to be with you because of your warm embrace,

I chose to be with you because you are a strong man,
I chose to be with you because you know how to stand in demand,

I chose to be with you because of your wittiness,
I chose to be with you because of your tenderness,

I chose to be with you because of your wisdom,
I chose to be with you because of your intelligence,

I chose to be with you because you encourage me,
I chose to be with you because you complete me,

I chose to be with you because you hold me,
I chose to be with you because you listened when no one else would,

I chose to be with you because you accepted me, for who I am,
I chose to be with you because you love me completely,

I chose to be with you because you never lied to me,
I chose to be with you because you took the lead and made me believe,

I chose to be with you because you are so smooth,
I chose to be with you because you don't lose your cool,

I chose to be with you because when we're together
you provide tranquility,

I chose to be with you because when we're together
you provide serenity,

Cont.

I chose to be with you because I love you,
I chose to be with you because our love is true,

"I chose to be with you because our souls are intertwined and we belong together"

A Mother & Daughter Memoirs of Love, Desire, Pain & Inspiration

"A Mother's Love"

Oh, the love of thy mother is like no other love at all,

She's wrapped around you like a blanket glued on you,

But when that presence disappears,

There's a void so wide,

So deep you fall in face first, like in a black hole and you're lost,

Someone has cut the lights out in your soul,

But fear not, because by God!

God's got it all under control,

Just when you think you can't take no more,

He throws strength right at you,

And, there comes another stepping stone,

To take you further in life,

Fret not my child,

"Just wait until we meet again someday"

"Arrow Of Explosion"

An arrow of explosion, is it love?

This arrow is going straight to the heart,

Deep down love is going straight through your veins,

How are you going to handle it?

Will you give in to the forces that be?

Or, will you run and hide, and stay inside your comfort zone,

This explosion is loud and hard,

The arrow is everywhere,

So, where are you going to go to feel the love?

Let go and give in!

This thing feels good; just watch your smile when everything is okay,

Let's do this love thing,

Swim with me in this watery pool of love!

"POW"

"Love Unconditionally"

What is love unconditionally?
Love unconditionally is the love you experience from God,
You don't understand yet you ask no questions,
You trust and believe in this unconditional love,
Now, you can receive love unconditionally from a
Being from this earth,
But, you can bet your bottom dollar it won't be the same,
Because, the love from this earth there is always some disbelief,
That one can't understand…this unconditional love!

"But God just keeps on loving you no matter what if you just believe"

"Me and My Girls"

Me and my girls is all I have,

They are true and blue,

But in the end that's all I have,

You would think, that they were in control sometimes the

way they look after me,

I know now that everyone is almost grown, and that

I've been blessed,

Sometimes their like having a bunch of little sisters and friends until

that motherly instinct kicks in,

"Thank you lord for my little girls"

A Mother & Daughter Memoirs of Love, Desire, Pain & Inspiration

"In The Right Side of My Heart"

When we fell in love,

You lit up my life,

I knew then that my heart was complete,

I need you to be strong for me,

So, I can continue to keep the beat of my heart strong,

Without you here with me at night,

I know that part of me can't rest,

So, come on now be strong for me,

So, we can be one at night together again,

I know God loves you and so do I,

So, I'm not ready to be without you not now,

So, fight this thing and come on home,

This place needs you not, but I need you a lot,

We still have things to do and places to go,

So, know that I'm waiting for you,

My heart is not whole without you here and neither is yours,

"So, let me help you become whole again"

"My Friends and Me"

My friends and me,

I try to be the best friend to have,

I am loving in every way,

I try to do all I'm asked of,

Just for my friends,

I have neat ones, sweet ones,

And loving ones who care,

But to be my friend you must be crazy as me,

They are good at times,

And sometimes they make me sick,

But, through it all, it comes down to my friends and me,

They range from all kinds,

Yes young, old, skinny, and fat,

We all have one thing in common,

We are looking to find the Lord in all that we do,

"My Friends and Me"

"The Beat of the Heart"

Two hearts beating to the same beat,

Oh, what a wonderful beat that must be,

The beat of two hearts beating as one,

Every beat never letting the sounds from outside

into the world of wonder,

Oh, what a peaceful harmony of love this must be,

A rhythm sound of music,

Sounding like beats in tune of each other's wants and needs,

Pound, pound oh! What a sound that must be,

If only, the sounds of happiness could last forever,

And, spread throughout the universe,

"Everything might be more pleasant and happy"

"My Dream"

When we met my heart felt a very special beat

That I never felt before,

Your spirit, just moved me in such a way,

That somehow, I knew we would have to be connected,

You are my friend and my love,

My dream come true,

There will be bad times and hard times too,

Just hang on in and come close,

Now close your eyes,

Because, my dream is to keep you mine,

To make you happy,

To keep you smiling at all times,

My dream is to keep you forever my lady,

So, lay quietly still and know that I love you today,

And tomorrow and forever,

Your spirit is so gentle,

So, let's grow old together,

And always be my dream come true,

"You are the other half of me, if you fall, I fall"

"The Little People"

Two Boys and Two Girls,

I could not ask for a better set of each,

They're little and smart and just as bright as can be,

They bother me, they worry me,

But I won't do without them,

They wait for me to come home from work to greet me with joy,

The moment that's over, they worry me to death,

They won't let me sleep; they won't let me eat,

All they think it's just me and them,

They treat me like there's no heaven or earth,

If I wasn't around,

The house is quiet and peaceful when they're not around,

"But it isn't the same unless I hear the sounds of little pitter patter and the sounds of their voices"

"My Full Size Luxury"

You're my Escalade, my Navigator,

The beauty of this thing called love,

It reminds me of your smell so new, so fresh,

Too comfortable to lean on,

It's so nice to be near you,

If I had known you way back when,

The joy we could've shared and

Spared each other some pain from our past,

You're my Escalade,

My Navigator the ride is so smooth except when

We hit a bump in the road and it could be over in a flash,

So, let's take the back roads,

The high roads and ride to the mountains

And leave everything behind.

"The wide open country roads are very smooth, so come play with me, ride with me, and live with me"

"My Precious Stones"

I have stones of love that are more precious to me
than just about anything can be,
My stones are my children and my grandchildren,
I love them all, for you lent them to me,
Lord God, I thank you!
I couldn't have asked for a more precious thing then
my stones of joy,
I have big ones and little ones,
Whose love I would not trade,
These stones are more precious than gold,
I know their mine just for a little while,
But please, Dear Lord make us strong,
You sent us an Angel to look after us,
Lord thank you for Mitch,
He means so much to us all,
He has become our shield to look after us,
And, knowing just when to say no,
My grandchildren are sweet two boys and two girls,
But, if you give me more I'll love them just as fine,

"To add to my Precious Stones"

A Mother & Daughter Memoirs of Love, Desire, Pain & Inspiration

"On This Day I Pledge"

On this day I pledge my love,

To you now and for always,

As we become one with one another,

One body,

One spirit,

And one soul,

When you hurt, I hurt,

When you cry, I cry,

Today, as we began this day together,

There is no more you or I,

But only "We" from now on,

Let us grow together,

We will let nothing break us apart,

I know your thoughts,

I know your answers…what you start I will finish,

If things get a little bad,

We will began to laugh,

Because, we fight for everything together from now on,

For God, has done great things,

And, we have come a long way,

Cont.

We grew together in Christ,
So, he bonded and welded our relationship for life,

"Now our love is like Noah's Ark…Strong but gentle to withstand the depths of time"

"The Day I Married"

Renita Toniece Parker,

Was married to someone on someday,

Year whatever,

They met some time ago,

I was surprised when it came to this,

But, I had been happy ever since,

The two of them are a team,

That was meant to be,

Some would have said it would have never worked,

But now, 15 years later they are just as content loving each other,

The friendship they had blossomed even more than before,

He couldn't ask for a better partner than that,

At first he thought this would never workout,

She has nothing to offer, So he thought!

They are now living in a Four Hundred Thousand Dollar House,

Just as happy as two peas in a pod,

"What a wonderful love story"

"We Are Connected"

You've come into my life like a cool breeze

blowing through a fall night,

Just when I needed someone,

I enjoyed being with you, and spending time with you,

I feel so comfortable just being next to you,

Who would have known, that we just met one another!

I feel as if I've known you for so long,

Don't get me wrong,

I'm not trying to smother you,

Or, trying to take all of your time,

But you must agree,

You must let life take its course,

Whatever is meant to be, it will all happen on its own,

"Because time is of the essence and we are so connected"

"Wedding"

On, this day we became one,

You became my friend,

My lover and my wife,

Through happiness heartaches and pain,

On this day not only in heart,

But in spirit as well,

This thing that God has done we vow together,

In front of everyone,

To let God's light shine through us,

For what he has done,

Now, let this poem be a part of me and a part of you,

Blessings and good friends are hard to come by,

But, when they do they last forever,

"My wife, my love to you on this Day"

Robin T. Dorsey & Renita T. Mock

A Mother & Daughter Memoirs of Love, Desire, Pain & Inspiration

2

*"Desire is the best temptation in the making,
That leaves you wanting more in anticipation"*

By: Robin T. Dorsey

"The Passion Between Us"

The passion between us was once so real,

The passion between us was never only a drill,

The passion between us was like a fairytale,

The passion between us was engaging and enduring,

The passion between us was sensational and inspirational,

The passion between us was devotional and emotional,

The passion between us was inviting and exciting,

The passion between us was tantalizing and mesmerizing,

The passion between us was secluded and eluded,

The passion between us was flirtatious and audacious,

The passion between us was hypnotic and erotic,

**"The passion between us we had a Blast but,
The passion between us went too Damn Fast"**

"Can I Have Some Of That"

Can I have some of that because I wanted it since we met,
Can I have some of that on my private jet,
Can I have some of that because you make it real wet,

Can I have some of that because it's looking kind of fat,
Can I have some of that because it is as big as a bat,
Can I have some of that because you do it good like that,

Can I have some of that because I want you to stick it in,
Can I have some of that because we can do it in the den,
Can I have some of that because I know we will get it in,

Can I have some of that because there's nothing that you lack,
Can I have some of that because last time you broke my back,
Can I have some of that because you are good in the sack,

"Thank you for hitting it from the back,
While giving me all of that"

"A Long Ride Home"

Riding home on a nice breezy night,
Listening to nice slow melodies
Driving slow so I can enjoy the moment,
Inspired by the sensual and sexy slow songs on the radio,
And, the nice breeze brushing up against my breast,
I begin to rub my thighs…
Rubbing my hands up and down my thighs nice and slow,
I began to go with the flow,
My hands then proceed to my inner thighs…
When I get there to my surprise,
I started to feel a warm tingling inside,
While the breeze brush against my breast,
Making my nipples tender to the touch,
I go back to my inner thighs,
Feeling very wet and warm inside,
While still driving I began to move my hips to the music,
Letting my fingers move in and out with the movement
Hmmmmmmmmmmmmm,
Feeling so good, I began to move faster,
Getting wet, wetter, and wetter,

Cont.

Now moaning to this intense pleasure,
Wondering what could be better…
My juices begin to drip, drip, and drip as I get wetter
As I exhale I noticed I'm home!
Still moaning from the momemt…

"An Intense Ride Was All the Way Home"

A Mother & Daughter Memoirs of Love, Desire, Pain & Inspiration

"Home Alone"

Laying at home,

All alone,

Wishing someone was here,

Lights are so bright,

So, I dim the lights,

Moving from room to room,

By candlelight,

Entering into the living room,

I turn on some sweet tunes,

Listening to the sweet slow melodies,

As my water drips into the tub,

Of my nice warm bubble bath,

With rose petals on top,

I un-button my shirt,

Take off my pants,

My bra, and my thong,

Stepping into my nice warm bath,

Submerging my body into the water,

While the bubbles, and rose petals cup my breast,

I begin to rub my legs, my thighs, and my Shhhhhhhhhhh,

Cont.

As my fingers begin to explore,
What's inside my inner thighs,
Rubbing oh so gently,
My nipples begin to harden,
Hmmmmmmm, that feels so good,
While my body temperature rise,
Because I'm caught up in the moment,
I pick up the phone to see,
Is this all it has to be…
A knock on the door,
So, I get out of the tub,
Dripping wet,
Anticipating each step,
As I open the door,
Immediately embraced,

"Home Alone Is No Longer The Case"

"Riding With My Mystery Man"

Tonight is the night,
When I'll be looking out of sight,
And my date will last all night,
The date will take all my might,
But, I will be alright,

Riding With My Mystery Man...

He came through at night,
To pick me up tonight,
He set the mood,
Smelling all good,
While playing slow jams,
We went to dinner and even a movie,
Enjoying each other's company,
But wait the best is yet to come,

Riding With My Mystery Man...

As we walk slowly to the car,
I turn to give him a hug,
Placing my soft breast into his chest,
With little sweet kisses on his neck,
We entered the car...
He sat in the driver seat,
While I sat in the back seat,
So, I can give him a little treat!

Riding With My Mystery Man...

He begins to drive slowly,
Wondering what's to come,
He adjusts his mirror,
To see what will be done,
Now, with all eyes on me...

Cont.

I slowly slip off my panties,
And lift up my dress,
Then I opened my legs,
So, he can see the rest,

Riding With My Mystery Man…

I started rubbing my kitty kat,
Making it wet, wet, and wetter,
Watching him watch me,
And feeling soooooooo good,
Is making me hot,
Still rubbing my wet kitty kat,
I close my eyes,
Moaning with pleasure,
Hmmmmmmmmm,

Riding With My Mystery Man…

I insert my finger in my kitty kat,
Moving it in,
And moving it out,
Telling him how good it feels,
Getting all nice and wet for him,

Riding With My Mystery Man…

We reach our destination,
And go inside,
Stopping at the first chair in sight,
I slip off my dress,
Then his clothes,

Cont.

So, I can rub his nice hard dick,
Making it harder and harder,
While I'm kissing his lips,
He sits in the chair,
And I sit on his lap,
And begin to ride,

This oh so intense pleasure,
Riding that dick,
While he grips my ass,
For more, more, and more,
Hmmm, he licked my nipples,
And sucked my breast,
Asking me who's the best,
In the heat of the moment,
We came together!

"Riding with my mystery man with all my might,
Giving it to him all through the night"

Robin T. Dorsey & Renita T. Mock

A Mother & Daughter Memoirs of Love, Desire, Pain & Inspiration

"You Unleashed the Freak"

You unleashed the *Freak,* and made me weak,
So, I couldn't even **SPEAK**!

You unleashed the *Freak,* and made me seek,
That overflowing **LEAK**!

You unleashed the *Freak,* and sent trimmers through my spine,
Now, I like it from **BEHIND**!

You unleashed the *Freak,* with all of that good meat,
Oh! What a **TREAT**!

You unleashed the *Freak,* when you made me your feast,
Damn, you are a **BEAST**!

You unleashed the *Freak,* I can't even sleep,
Because I'm in too **Deep**!

You unleashed the *Freak,* I couldn't even answer a call,
Because, you had me climbing the **Walls**!

You unleashed the *Freak,* now I need a glass of wine,
Because, you said you were **Mine**!

You unleashed the *Freak,* and made me say, **Oh Daddy**, can you stay all day, 'Cause I want to play in the **Hay**!

**"Now, that the Freak is unleashed,
Oh, what an incredible release"**

"You Make Me Feel Like"

You make me feel like the luckiest girl in the world,
You make me feel like sipping on margarita swirls,
You make me feel like a unique little pearl,

You make me feel like screaming to the mountain tops,
You make me feel like hopping until I can't stop,
You make me feel like singing until I want to drop,

You make me feel like cooking some shake-n-bake,
You make me feel like cake for goodness sake,

You make me feel like being with you exclusively,
You make me feel like we will be together effusively,
You make me feel like this is the real deal, and
I don't want anybody else,

"When we are together the whole planet stops and the earth shakes…All because you make me feel like"

"Oh Yes"

The way you look at me makes me smile…Oh Yes,

The way you speak is as smooth as the Nile…Oh Yes,

The way you smell like I knew you would…Oh Yes,

The way you hold me feels so good…Oh Yes,

The way you kiss me makes me weak…Oh Yes,

The way you made me your little freak…Oh Yes,

The way you caress me send chills up my spine…Oh Yes,

The way you love me makes me weep…Oh Yes,

The way you spank me with your belt…Oh Yes,

The way you lift me up and how you made me felt…Oh Yes,

The way you lick it makes me melt…Oh Yes,

The way you made me cum you said it taste like rum…Oh Yes,

The way you stuck it in and it didn't bend…Oh Yes,

The way you hit it in from north, south, east to west…Oh Yes,

"The way you made me scream your name makes me say… Oh Yes"

"Why All Of Me"

I know that I can be all the woman you want me
to be but why all of me,
The things we have together are so deep,
You keep trying to get it all out of me,
But, love that deep and that strong,
And oh so sweet, and now you say you want all of me,
It's a flight that I'm afraid of not knowing where it will take me,
Are you already there, Baby it's real I know because I feel all of you,
I have so much to offer you but in turn I want all of you,
You are my lover, my soul's desire,
Let's go to Cancun and live like there isn't no tomorrow, and let our
Bodies' come together and receive each other,
Let our souls connect as one,
You are what I need and I'll be there for you,

**"Last with me forever, let our dreams be the same because
You'll have…All of me"**

"Sex"

Sex to me is like a drug,
If you have never had it you will never miss it,
But once you get that fuel injection,
Your body becomes its own,
You want it even when you don't think about it,
But one thing is for sure,
The older you get the better you are to handle it,
Once, you fall in love with that one special love,
Then love becomes a thing of beauty,
So good, that in this moment you become one with another,
But if you're young you seem to think this is so good,

"But it's only SEX"

Robin T. Dorsey & Renita T. Mock

A Mother & Daughter Memoirs of Love, Desire, Pain & Inspiration

3

"Pain is the pit in your stomach that leaves you feeling numb after you have done all you can do"

By: Robin T. Dorsey

"Day Dreamer"

I always tried to be with you…but you didn't believe in me,

I always tried to be with you…but you always gave

me a hard way to go,

I always tried to be with you…but you constantly told me no,

I always tried to be with you…but you tried to play hard to get,

I always tried to be with you…but you went to another,

I always tried to be with you…but you were always

trying to be my mother,

I always tried to be with you…but you

wouldn't love a brother,

I always tried to be with you…but you said the

hood was my friend,

I always tried to be with you…but I had a few

babies in the end,

**"I will always love you until the day I die,
Because true love will one day prevail"**

"Despite Of"

Despite of...You told me I couldn't yet I did,

Despite of...You didn't believe in me so I had to believe in myself,

Despite of...Your negativity I only projected positivity,

Despite of...You told me dreams are not real...But yet you can't afford a meal,

Despite of...You didn't give me love and now you want to be loved,

Despite of...You tried to hold me back but I finally found my knack,

Despite of...You said you had my back only to found out later that you are whack,

Despite of...You wanted me to cut you some slack now I have turned my back,

Despite of...You were always in the sack and yet you always got caught in the act,

Despite of...You think you are so bold yet people only think of you as cold,

Despite of...You asked me out on a date but you was too much of a flake,

"Despite of my past...I realized my dreams and I am accomplishing my task"

"Can You Handle It"

You said you needed me,
You said you loved me,
Can you handle it...

You said you wanted to be with me,
But, you don't have time for me,
Can you really handle it...

We fuss,
We fight,
With all our might,
Is this how you really want it,
Can you handle it...

Today,
Tonight,
Can we make things alright?
Can we try to promise not another lonely night?
Can you handle it...

We cry,
We laugh,
We make it past,
We have a blast,
We make love at last,
But, how long will it last,
Putting time to the task,
Can you handle it...

Cont.

Now, what should we do?
Make time for it,
Deal with it,
Or, just forget it,

"How do you want to handle it"

"Can I Wait To See"

If it's really meant to be,

If it's me you want it to be,

Waiting and wondering is it me,

Asking you who will it be,

Do you love thee?

Not getting a reply,

So, I decide to move on,

Then you come around,

Always trying to get it on,

So I wonder,

Could this be,

Do you really want to be with me,

Moments later you embrace,

From the love you have shown in my face,

Although times are good,

And times are bad,

When they're bad you're always sad,

Not dealing with the problems,

So, you turn to another,

Wanting her to be your lover,

Now, she's your lover,

But you're undercover,

Trying to hide your lover from me,

Acting like I can no longer see,

Cont.

The changes you have shown me,

Still loving you endlessly,

You come back to me,

Still loving me,

Leaving her to be,

Only to tell me,

You care about me,

Never confessing your love for me,

Because you're scared to commit,

So, you only try to love me a little bit,

Your heart say's I do,

Your mind say's I won't,

Together at last,

Forgetting about the past,

See, we have fun at last,

There will come a time to be,

Where you will have to see,

A choice has to be made,

Will you marry me,

Or, walk away and just be,

Without me,

Be true to you,

Be true to me,

"Be true to the Love you have for Thee!"

"Don't Try to Control Me"

Don't try to control me…because I am a free spirit,

Don't try to control me…because I am living my dream,

Don't try to control me…because how I live

my life works for me,

Don't try to control me…because life is too short only to dream,

Don't try to control me…because it makes me want to scream,

Don't try to control me…because my love is like a beam,

Don't try to control me…because I will

fall through the seams,

Don't try to control me…because I don't want to be mean,

Don't try to control me…because my goals are extreme,

Don't try to control me…because my destiny will be pristine and

has already been deemed!

"Life is about choices not chances, live your dreams and don't let anyone stand in your way of your destiny"

"People Will Let You Down"

People will let you down…If you give them a chance to,
People will let you down…If you put your faith in their hands
to hurt you,
People will let you down…If you trust them
to help you,
People will let you down…If you believe their
love is true,
People will let you down…If you allow them to
get near you,
People will let you down…If you appear to be
real weak too,
People will let you down…If you let
them clown you,
People will let you down…If you bow down to
their will too,
People will let you down…If you are
always too fearful,
People will let you down…If you are
too real too,
People will let you down…If you
are too cheerful,

"People will let you down…If you give them the will to"

A Mother & Daughter Memoirs of Love, Desire, Pain & Inspiration

"That's That Bullsh*t"

You say you need me in your life but nothing seems right,

That's that Bullsh*t,

You licked it but won't stick it, That's that Bullsh*t,

You Fuck me and then duck me, That's that Bullsh*t,

You got me screaming your name when you bring the pain but it's all in vain, That's that Bullsh*t,

You befriend me and then unfriend me,

That's that Bullsh*t,

You bet me for my drawers but you don't have no balls,

That's that Bullsh*t,

You lied to me and acted like it was true,

That's that Bullsh*t,

You were caught in the act so your Ass is whack,

That's that Bullsh*t,

We had a date but you came to my house late, That's that Bullsh*t,

You said I got bait but now you want to hate, That's that Bullsh*t,

I texted you at 10:00 but you texted me back at 4:00 am,

That's that Bullsh*t,

You are my mate but couldn't pay for my plate,

That's that Bullsh*t,

You stayed out late yet you haven't even ate, That's that Bullsh*t,

You claim you bought me but you can't support me,

That's that Bullsh*t,

Cont.

You found me from afar and said we would go far,

Then you ran me over with your car,

That's that Bullsh*t,

You always at the bar yet you don't have a car,

That's that Bullsh*t,

You are in the club making it rain, but your kids are living in vain,

That's that Bullsh*t,

You live at home with your mama and got baby mama drama,

That's that Bullsh*t,

You brag about swag, and talk about things you ain't never had,

That's that Bullsh*t,

You say you go long, but you don't last past a three minute song,

That's that Bullsh*t,

You say you need a babysitter but never come back to get her,

That's that Bullsh*t,

You never pick-up your phone but we all know you home,

That's that Bullsh*t,

You want me to be your wife when the liquor is flowing right but on a sober night things don't be right,

That's that Bullsh*t,

You stay out all Damn night then call me crazy when I pull out the knife, That's that Bullsh*t,

"The love I thought we shared inspired me, and I wanted more but now it's too late and I am walking out the door. I had enough of this Bullsh*t"

"Time To Walk Away"

Time to walk away…to start a new beginning,
Time to walk away…because our love is ending,
Time to walk away…because I no longer want to stay,
Time to walk away…because I am tired
of having things your way,
Time to walk away…because you didn't have much to say,
Time to walk away…so I may live another day,
Time to walk away…because you kept me at bay,
Time to walk away…because I missed you every day,
Time to walk away…because all you want to do is play,
Time to walk away…because you didn't ask me to stay,

"Time to walk away…so I can live my life day after day"

"You Said You Had My Back"

You said you had my back…but now I know you are whack,

You said you had my back…but you only wanted to

focus on what I lacked,

You said you had my back…but yet you don't have jack,

You said you had my back…but you was only here to mack,

You said you had my back…but you only wanted to get me in the sack,

You said you had my back…but your intentions wasn't real,

You said you had my back…but all you ate was my meals,

You said you had my back…but you

couldn't help with the bills,

You said you had my back…but you took my damn wheels,

You said you had my back…but you was only a cheap thrill,

"Now, I am turning my back…so how you like that"

"You Are A Liar"

You say one thing and do another because,

You are a Liar,

You cheat and you steal because,

You are a Liar,

Your knees get weak and you barely speak because,

You are a Liar,

You swept me off my feet and made me weep because,

You are a Liar,

You held another when you were my lover because,

You are a Liar,

You wanted me to nurture, but you knew we had no future because,

You are a Liar,

You are a part of my past, but now you want to make it last because,

You are a Liar,

You said you was real but now I know the deal because,

You are a Liar,

You hurt me so bad which made me very mad,

You Dirty Little Liar,

"Your Lies have FAILED now I will PREVAIL so be GONE …YOU NO GOOD LIAR"

"Why Are You So Selfish"

You have been blessed by the best so,

Why are you so Selfish,

You live a good life and fought a good fight so,

Why are you so Selfish,

You are blessed to have a mother when some have no other so,

Why are you so Selfish,

You live in the land of the free but yet you only want to smoke on trees so, Why are you so Selfish,

You have a daughter, son, and wife but you don't want that life,

Why are you so Selfish,

You have a mansion on the hill but you won't pay the bills,

Why are you so Selfish,

You took her for granted when she was trying to be romantic,

Why are you so Selfish,

You spent all of the money and wondering why you can't get no honey,

Why are you so Selfish,

"When are you going to stop being so Selfish and enjoy your blessings"

A Mother & Daughter Memoirs of Love, Desire, Pain & Inspiration

"You Thought I Would Fail"

You thought I would fail…so now I am going to prevail,

You thought I would fail…so now it is time for you to bail,

You thought I would fail…but I am a resilient woman,

You thought I would fail…but I am a warrior,

You thought I would fail…but I am a provider,

You thought I would fail…but I don't even

know the meaning of failure,

You thought I would fail…but I only needed closure,

You thought I would fail…but I only wanted to yell,

You thought I would fail…but you wanted me to pay your bail,

You thought I would fail…but you still sending me emails,

You thought I would fail…but your ass just went to jail,

You thought I would fail…so why you look so pale,

"Failure is not an option when you are determined to WIN"

"I Thought You Loved Me"

I thought you loved me…when you asked for me to stay,

I thought you loved me…but you made me walk away,

I thought you loved me…but you only wanted to play,

I thought you loved me…but you simply wanted your way,

I thought you loved me…but you never made the time of day,

I thought you loved me…but you kept me at bay,

I thought you loved me…but you refused to show your love,

I thought you loved me…but you wouldn't let me in,

I thought you loved me…but you treated our love as

if it was a sin,

I thought you loved me…and our love would last

through thick and thin,

I thought you loved me…but you couldn't communicate

time and time again,

I thought you loved me…but you choose to ignore me in the end,

"Because you wouldn't love me I choose to walk away, and it's too late for you to ask me to STAY"

"In Care of My Child"

You think your life is so hard,

But you have just begun to live,

You think you have the worst mother in the world,

Although, I know you don't want to understand it's all out of love,

I hope the mistakes we make as people don't hinder our love,

Before it's too late to show it to one another,

We don't choose our parents or our children,

But we only get one shot at one mother and one father,

Many people can try to take the place of them,

But no one will love you like a mother will,

You will one day become a mother and I hope you put

your best foot forward,

Good luck in the world my darling child,

"I hope you come around before I'm gone, and it's not too late to know we are a TEAM"

"The Life of an Officer"

Oh, if you only knew the other side of the wall of the
life of an Officer,
It's strange, it's dangerous, it's intense, and it's exciting,
You don't even know what the next day will hold,
Will you survive or will you be next?
It's like playing a game of chess,
One minute you're high on the excitement,
The next time you don't know where the fear came in,
But you know it's there.
People being stabbed, robbed, and raped and there's
nothing you can do!
Without trying to get caught up in this crazy mixed up world.

"Living the Life of an Officer"

A Mother & Daughter Memoirs of Love, Desire, Pain & Inspiration

"It Just Doesn't Matter"

It doesn't matter what you think of me,

Or, what you think I should be,

Because this is not your life to live,

It's mine to live for the Heavenly Father, whom I must please,

You can't stop me from getting into heaven,

You can't save me from anything,

Not death or happiness,

You won't be able to open up the pearly white gates,

So, it doesn't matter what you think of me,

I'm not here to please you,

I could make you happy and have fun too,

But you, yourself have said it better than me,

I can't do anything for you,

I'm not the one,

So you say but you know what,

You don't have to beat me in the head with a brick anymore,

Because, this old floor mat is all worn out,

Do what you do best,

Kick me to the curb just one last time,

It was fun while it lasted,

But it's going nowhere fast.

"You have just shut it down when it comes to me and you"

"In Time"

In time things happen, and we haven't

even planned for it that way,

Now, let me make your day,

Be as bright as the morning sun,

I'm your friend until death do us part,

No matter what,

I know you don't feel that bubbling over in love thing for me,

But, trust in me when I say happiness, it's right at your side,

What if one lousy day comes and you finally say,

I didn't even know that I was in love with you in anyway,

But until you see,

What's out there or shall I say what's not out there,

You'll never know,

Because, the love and understanding that we share,

Can never be found again anywhere,

You trust me, we talk,

The Chemistry is all that,

I know that you love me even more than you say,

Because, I feel the emotions whenever we're together,

Just stop shutting down and let me in,

Whatever it is that keeps you from total commitment,

I don't know,

Stop seeing my flaws,

And see how I can be for you,

Cont.

If it's in God's plans for us to be one,
You would never regret loving me for life,
Pride is what you had,
But I'm what you have,
In God's plan happiness and a peace of mind.

"I'm just letting go and letting God"

"The Midnight Hour"

It's the silent time of life in which we all should let

our souls rest in peace,

But that's not so,

There is life still moving,

People going places,

Doing things,

Works going on much to your dismay you know there's

confusion in the world,

Because it's too much going on,

It's lonely even when there are people around,

Life is a strange thing it's like living while you're dead

or dead while you're living,

There's sorrow,

Pain and all kinds of things going on in the

midnight hour of our life,

But don't be short,

Because, sure enough through all that's happening there's loving going

on in the midnight hour,

Kids pretending to be grown and don't know what's going on

in this crazy mixed up world,

"Life is strange in the midnight hour of our life"

"The Pain of Love"

You were my love,

My life; we thought we had what it took to be the perfect mates,

Two souls separated by fate,

On the pain of love no matter what happen,

We tried our best to hold it all together;

One lost and one soul searching for peace and harmony

in which the other couldn't help,

Because he was lost himself,

There could have been much to gain,

But, the pain of love was just so deep there was no way out,

You were my friend I needed that,

And I thank you for that,

Please dear love, know that I love you,

But, I couldn't help you out of that hole you fell in,

You hurt me so deep down inside, and I fell into a hole myself,

But to your dismay,

I found my way out and now it's over!

Never to begin again,

"Oh, the pain of Love is so very DEEP"

"Winter Months"

Winter months are such pretty ones,
The colors change the trees,
Sometimes, they go bear with nothing on them,
It's so quiet that you hardly hear any noises at all,
Now, you would think it's the perfect season for
sharing your love with someone,
But just as it may be, and you don't have any problems,
Yet, it seems like you're all alone,
And all you can hear is the wind blowing outside,
No one to hold on too,
Then you realize that it's winter,
No hussle, no bussle just you and your thoughts,
Left alone to ponder all by yourself,
"What will the winter months hold for you?
It's cold and brisk,
It's dark early and it's very lonely,
During the three months it's here,
You would have thought it was at least six months or long,
I need you here so I won't be alone,

"So, love me always during these Winter Months"

Robin T. Dorsey & Renita T. Mock

"Wondering What"

Do you ever wonder what your friends and family think

when they constantly ask,

Would you, could you?

Please take me here,

Take me there,

If you could please do this or do that,

I don't care if you say no but,

I know that you will not and I'll say thank you,

Not ever wondering that maybe I should do more,

Or, give you something,

Just because you're always taking me here and taking me there,

And doing that without ever asking for anything from us,

Maybe here I'll give you a token here's a $20 or a $10,

You could at least just send me a card,

Or, just say let me do something just for you,

"Do you ever wonder what in the world are they thinking"

4

Inspiration

"To be inspired and being able to make a difference is the most rewarding key to life. All things are possible if you just believe"

By: Robin T. Dorsey

"A Path"

A path is your road map to success,

A path is what sets you apart from the rest,

A path is when you do your very best,

A path is a mess that allowed you to pass the test,

A path is your soul and eternal rest,

A path is a ticket to your future's best,

A path will allow you to put your faith to the test,

A path will show you that you are truly the best,

A path will let people know that you are not pressed,

A path will bring you out of your mess with finesse,

A path will show you who the best is,

"A path will show you can be as good as the REST"

"Always There"

When I need you,
You are always there!

When I'm sad,
You are always there!

When I need a shoulder to cry on,
You are always there!

When I'm sick,
You are always there!

When I need an ear,
You are always there!

When I'm hungry,
You are always there!

When I need a place to stay,
You are always there!

You are always there when I need you,
No matter if it is a storm or a tide,
You are always there!

**"I wanted to let you know how special you are
to me and I'm always here for you,**

**And to tell you how much I love and appreciate you
through the good and the bad"**

A Mother & Daughter Memoirs of Love, Desire, Pain & Inspiration

"Do You Believe"

Do you believe in you?

Do you believe in me?

Do you believe in we?

Do you believe in is it meant to be?

Do you believe in he?

Do you believe in just wait and see?

Do you believe in your will?

Do you believe in just chill?

Do you believe in the pill?

Do you believe in the thrill?

Do you believe in deals?

Do you believe in hills?

Do you believe in paying your bills?

Do you believe in love?

Do you believe in doves?

"Whatever you believe in just keep it real and in the end You will truly win"

"If I Don't Make It Past Tomorrow"

Not knowing where I'll be,

Serving time on this earth,

Trying to find out who could I be,

I thought, living, loving and learning,

How hard could that be,

To only find out it's just me,

With nowhere to run,

Or, even try to turn to,

Looking all around,

To see who's around you,

Remembering oh,

There is one above you,

Not realizing that he said he'll never leave you,

Turning around standing to my feet,

Hearing him say…I can't be beat,

Tomorrow's not promised,

Count your blessing today,

With Grace, Love, and Mercy,

What else could there be,

**"Love today,
Don't worry about another da."**

"Friends"

Friends are about building relationships,
No matter what the reason is,
When a friend comes into your life,
A friend can change your life,
Whether good or bad,
A friend is someone who has your back,
Who lends an ear when you need it,
Who lends a shoulder to help you cry on it,
Who lends you money when you don't have it,
A friend is understanding, patient,
Caring, and kind,
A friend should not be taken for granted,
Because, a friend will be there until the end,

But a ***True Friend***,
Will tell you the truth when you,
Want to hear a lie,
A true friend has unconditional love for you,
Despite your faults,
Or your flaws,
A True Friend will weather the storm,
Even if they are to blame,
A true friend will stay and work it out,
And at the end you both will stand!
My question to you is simple…
Do you have a Friend?
Or, better yet a ***True Friend?***

**"Or, are you too caught up on you,
And Still Don't Have Any Friends"**

Robin T. Dorsey & Renita T. Mock

"The Day You Were Born"

The day you were born…they told me it's a boy,
The day you were born…It brought me so much joy!

The day you were born…you changed my life forever,
The day you were born…I knew you would be very clever,

The day you were born…you became my life,
The day you were born…you brightened up my life!

The day you were born…you made me realize
how precious life is,
The day you were born…I couldn't believe you belonged to me,
The day you were born…you taught me the true meaning of
how to love thee,
The day you were born…you truly loved me,
The day you were born…I knew it was truly meant to be!

**"The day you were born…you was the apple of my eye,
I will always love you until the day I DIE"**

A Mother & Daughter Memoirs of Love, Desire, Pain & Inspiration

"I Strive"

I strive to be the best that I can be,

I strive to always be true to me,

I strive to live life stress free,

I strive to love unconditionally,

I strive to fulfill my destiny,

I strive to be the best mother anyone could be,

I strive to be debt free,

I strive to follow God's plan for me,

I strive to motivate another,

I strive to have peace when I sleep,

I strive not to fall in too deep,

I strive not to judge anyone's past,

I strive to make friendships last,

I strive to be a pillar in my community,

I strive to bring togetherness and unity,

I strive to live, love, and have purity,

I strive to make a difference in the world,

I strive to see my dreams come to past,

I strive to live life and have a blast,

**"Strive for the best and watch God do the rest,
For when you strive you have a future to look forward to"**

"Dreams Do Come True"

I once was a dreamer but now I am a Believer that,

Dreams do come true,

I am an achiever and know that,

Dreams do come true,

I have set goals and met goals because,

Dreams do come true,

I am a conqueror and know that,

Dreams do come true,

I was told I couldn't or I wouldn't but,

Dreams do come true,

I have been disappointed and now I am anointed that,

Dreams do come true,

I have cried many times and spent my last dime but,

Dreams do come true,

I have been lied to and they tried to break my spirits but,

Dreams do come true,

I have had my heart broken but,

Dreams do come true,

I have failed many times but,

Dreams do come true,

I have a dream to succeed so I know that, Dreams do come true,

"Dreams Do Come True as long as you believe in God and yourself to know that the opportunities are endless…now go and make it happen"

"My Goal"

My goal is to be me,

My goal is to be set free,

My goal is to live life debt free,

My goal is to be all that I can be,

My goal is to live worry free,

My goal is to always be honest to me,

My goal is to give unconditionally,

My goal is to work for me totally,

My goal is to live spiritually,

My goal is to love completely,

My goal is to teach my son to be the man that he can be,

"My goal is to be true to thee"

"I Was Broken"

I was broken…because you used me as a shield,

I was broken…because I didn't know how to yield,

I was broken…because I was living too freely on this earth,

I was broken…because I didn't know my own worth,

I was broken…because I didn't know how to cope,

I was broken…because I had given up on hope,

I was broken…because I needed to pause for the cause,

I was broken…because I never knew what true love was,

I was broken…because I loved everyone else more,

I was broken…because you were a little whore,

I was broken…because all I wanted to do was work,

I was broken…because you were a jerk,

I was broken…because I loved you despite of your flaws,

I was broken…because I didn't have any balls,

I was broken…because I wouldn't let you in,

I was broken…because I was living in sin,

I was broken…because my heart wouldn't allow me to bend,

I was broken…because it was too hard to mend,

I was broken…because I couldn't contend,

I was broken…but now I am revealed,

I was broken…but now I am healed

**"Being broken is not a means to an end;
Being broken is the way to begin again"**

"Living Life & Loving It"

I am a **Daughter** and I am Living Life & Loving It,

I am a **Mother** and I am Living Life & Loving It,

I am a **Sister** and I am Living Life & Loving It,

I am a **Poet** and I am Living Life & Loving It,

I am a **True Friend** and I am Living Life & Loving It,

I am a **Romantic** and I am Living Life & Loving It,

I am a **Healer** and I am Living Life & Loving It,

I am a **Speaker** and I am Living Life & Loving It,

I am an **Educator** and I am Living Life & Loving It,

I am a **Motivator** and I am Living Life & Loving It,

I am an **Inspiration** and I am Living Life & Loving It,

I am an **Advocate** and I am Living Life & Loving It,

I am a **Life Coach** and I am Living Life & Loving It,

I am an **Achiever** and I am Living Life & Loving It,

I am a **Believer** and I am Living Life & Loving It,

I am a **Woman of God** and I am Living Life & Loving It,

I am a **Blessing** and I am Living Life & Loving It,

I am a **Survivor** and I am Living Life & Loving It,

Cont.

I am a **Socialite** and I am Living Life & Loving It,

I am a **Goal Setter** and I am Living Life & Loving It,

I am a **Trendsetter** and I am Living Life & Loving It,

I am a **Philanthropist** and I am Living Life & Loving It,

I am a **Person** who stands up for what I believe in and

I am Living Life & Loving It,

**"My name is Robin Dorsey and I am a Mother, an Author, a Motivational Speaker, and an Entrepreneur and
I am Living Life & Loving It"**

A Mother & Daughter Memoirs of Love, Desire, Pain & Inspiration

"Procrastination"

Stop procrastinating and put your plan into action,
Stop procrastinating and complaining and make it happen,
Stop procrastinating and feeling sorry for yourself
and love yourself,
Stop procrastinating because you're waiting for
someone else to do your job,
Stop procrastinating and stand up and be the woman or
man God chose you to be,
Stop procrastinating and thinking about what could be,
So you can be all that you can be,
Stop procrastinating and screaming about your past when you can
make your dreams come true at last,
Stop procrastinating because you have what it takes,
For goodness sakes,
Stop procrastinating about the pain because it is driving you insane,
Stop procrastinating because say you don't know what to do,
Because you can always find a way,
Stop procrastinating because you are a gem indeed
and you can succeed,
Stop procrastinating because in order to win,
You have to find a way to begin,

"Procrastination is the root of the problem and can cause your destiny to be unfilled, and you are who the Lord has made so take action and make him proud"

"God Chose Me"

God chose me…because he loved me,

God chose me…because he knew what I would be,

God chose me…because he saw the best in me,

God chose me…because he knew I could lead thee,

God chose me…because he knew I could make a difference,

God chose me…because he knew I couldn't be indifferent,

God chose me…because he knew I was gentle,

God chose me…because he knew I was so sentimental,

God chose me…because he knew I was passionate,

God chose me…because he knew I was compassionate,

God chose me…because he knew I believed in him,

"God chose me because; I am a Child of God"

"A Day of Thanksgiving"

On this nice beautiful fall day,

God has chosen to send a blessing for everyone,

Your 1st blessing as you arise from your sleep,

Still knowing who you are,

2nd you still have all of the material blessings you had yesterday,

3rd and some of us still have our loved ones near,

But even so God is still standing there,

In case you get tired and can't walk no more,

"He will lift you up and take away your burdens"

##

Flowers are bright,

Flowers are light,

Flowers are forever,

Flowers can help you be together,

Flowers are of love…all set up in a bouquet,

Flowers are for you,

Flowers are for me,

Flowers are here to set you free,

Flowers are beautiful,

Flowers are thoughtful,

Flowers are meaningful,

Flowers represent friendship,

Flowers represent love,

Flowers represent romance,

Flowers represent passion,

Flowers represent a window through our soul,

"I love flowers and I love YOU"

Oh, what a powerful being he is,
If you don't know then you just
need to know,
For your life will depend on you knowing him,
You just should know how blessed you are,
Without even trying real hard,
God is the almighty God,
He has created so many things and at the same time he
can take it all away,
He has, he is the power of the world,

"Nothing is done without Him"

"Happiness"

Happiness is now my future,

I'm so glad that I've found peace in my soul,

Happiness is wonderful,

Happiness is good to have,

God, has blessed me with a peace of mind and faith so strong even in the darkest hour,

I look to the Lord and I'm overwhelmed with this happiness I seem to find,

I'm happily in love,

I'm happy with my children and with my life,

Have prayer and believe in your faith in God,

Makes everything alright,

I try to teach my kids if you find peace in Christ everything will be alright,

"And happiness is just a step away"

"Heaven Help Us"

Lord, heaven help us,

We're in the dog days of time,

Kids are disrespecting their parents,

Kids killing kids,

Kids killing their parents,

We are trying to do the best that we can do,

And, they don't want to believe in anything that's right,

Lord, they want to learn the hard way,

Which is the wrong way of life,

They are dying young and don't even realize it's their

life on the line for real,

Lord, heaven help us all,

For we know not what we are doing,

It's all like a growing process,

We need to be strong in faith,

Let our actions show in thy words,

"We do, Lord, heaven help us ALL"

Robin T. Dorsey & Renita T. Mock

"I'm Free"

"Don't Cry" for me,

For I'm not "Lost",

I know you're hurt because it was "Too Soon",

Maybe too early on in my life,

But you know "My Father" Loves Me More,

So, I had to leave for it was my time to go,

You see "My Father" here has a "Mansion", where he said I had a

room now just "Stay Calm" and

I'll wait until you meet me here in this "New Life",

Be good to one another for kindness is the "Key",

Pray for me "No More" because now "I'll Pray for You",

While I wait to see you again,

Remember and laugh at all the joys we shared,

Pass on my "Smile" and be slow to speak and

quick to listen because

someone here will need you more,

Because, when you see the birds in the sky just know, that

"This Dove Took Flight & I'm Flying Up High",

You know that I love you and I'll "Always be watching over you",

Now rest in "Peace" Friends & Family, I'm "Okay",

"In My Father's House"

"It's Up To You"

If you really want to be a great success…It's up to you,

Or, if you choose to do less than your best…It's up to you,

Whether you'll be flying high, or only barely getting by,

I'm just here to clarify that…It's up to you,

If you're to overcome your problems,

There's no doubt…It's up to you,

Whether you'll enjoy great fame,

You'll have no one else to blame because…It's clearly up to you,

When the heat is on, you ask what can I say…It's up to you,

Are you willing to pay the price you have to pay…It's up to you,

Whether you'll do something great,

Or, only just procrastinate…It's up to you,

Yes, I'm concerned about your fate, but…It's positively up to you,

There's absolutely no limit to what you can do but…It's up to you,

Do you have the guts; the will to follow through…It's up to you,

Whether your fire gets lit,

Or, whether you decide to quit…It's up to you,

Worrying about it won't help one bit because…It's really up to you,

Just how far will you really go "Who knows"…It's up to you,

Whether the crop you've planted grows and grows…It's up to you,

Whether you "Score" with the ball,

Fumble it, or worse, miss the call…It's clearly up to you,

Oh, you can have all that life can give,

But can't you see…It's up to you,

Cont.

If you're fed up with your lifestyle,
Don't look at me…It's up to you,
Whether you succeed or fail,
Get to Heaven or Burn in Hell,
How many times will I have to say that?

**"It's positively, Absolutely, Undeniably, Inescapably…
IT'S UP TO YOU"**

"Living"

Living is a good thing,

Pain is a teacher,

Pain can bring wisdom,

You didn't know you had,

Living is to be mastered,

To be blossomed,

And then we wither for a time of new growth,

Living can be so long,

We seem to hang on,

And then there are times where living is not long enough,

We wonder where did the time go just yesterday,

I was little for now I'm old,

Living can be lonely and living can be crowded,

With all so many people,

Living has a means and means has an ending,

"But where there's an end there is a new beginning"

"Time is Near"

Time is near,

So, you better get ready because…time is coming,

You need to be aware that…time is near,

So, find your peace in the heavenly father,

There is death and grief among us…because time is near,

Bow down, on your knees and make peace if you please,

Cause our father is coming to claim all his children…because time is near,

You need to love one another…because time is near,

Please take time to say thank you Lord,

You better get ready…because time is near,

You need to know which way you are going or coming…because time is near,

"Please find your peace now…because time is near"

"When I Go Home"

When I go home to be with my Lord don't cry, don't fret,
For, I have lived a good life,
Fought a good fight, now it's time to move on,
Do what you have to, so I'll see you again,
Don't let the worries of the world get you down, this life here
is only temporary,
I loved every one of you, who touch my soul,
No matter what happen between us,
At some point and time all is forgiven and all is not lost,
I've moved on and so must you,
When I go home, I'm going in peace to sleep awhile until
"He" returns for everyone,
As you know in my writings, my saying is "Peace be Still",
Now, ride the waves but hang on tight,
Tears cometh in the night, but joy comes in the morning,
Now, take care because I'm sure I'll see you again and
I'll watch you from afar
with careful eyes, love, peace and happiness,

"In loving care, your mother, your sister, your wife, your friend"

"You Can't Stop"

You can't stop the flow of things,

But, when it happens it will proceed just the way it's supposed to be,

No matter what the turn of events,

We know prayer helps,

We know "He" hears,

But, what we don't want to believe is,

"His" will to do as He please,

He said you have the power to change the things you're allowed to,

But, you must accept the things that you can't change,

Some things are simply meant to be,

"And we should just stop and give thanks"

"If I Could Do It Over"

If I could do it over again,

I would do it all the same,

Because, the life lessons that I have learned through good

times and hard ones too,

Has made me the person or the woman that I am today,

Struggle is worship,

To have struggled will make you go to God in prayer,

To have lived will make you strong,

There should be no regrets in life,

Because, we come from a pre-destined God who knows

the beginning and the end,

He knows the outcome for every one of us,

So, to know Him is to believe in Him,

These things I have gone through has made me one of you,

A strong survivor of life,

A motivator of words,

I hope my thoughts touch yours so we can be spiritually

as one body and one soul,

Learn from your mistakes, it will take you far.

"AMEN"

A MOTHER & DAUGHTER MEMOIRS OF
LOVE, DESIRE, PAIN & INSPIRATION

ABOUT THE AUTHORS

Robin T. Dorsey

Robin T. Dorsey is a native of Washington, DC/Maryland. She is an extraordinary motivational speaker, entrepreneur, philanthropist, mother, and author. Ms. Dorsey has always been driven to reach the highest mountains. She attributes being able to accomplish the goals that she set and met to her mother who always encouraged her to live her dreams and to be all that she could be. Her father "Robert A. Dorsey" always taught her if you work hard you can achieve anything. Ms. Dorsey has been featured in numerous publications, and she is currently pursuing her PhD in Philosophy/Business. She is "Living Life & Loving It".

Renita T. Mock

Renita T. Mock was born in Washington, DC. She was a true pioneer of all times. She was an amazing woman who gave endlessly up until her two year battle with Stage 4 Breast Cancer ended her life. She was a courageous woman, a motivator, a mother, and a true friend. She leaves behind her words of wisdom through her poetry. It was Ms. Mock's life dream to be a published author so her legacy could live forever.

To learn more about these incredible women visit:
www.dorseypublishing.com & www.robindorsey.com

A MOTHER & DAUGHTER
MEMOIRS OF
LOVE, DESIRE, PAIN
& INSPIRATION

www.DorseyPublishing.com

www.ingramcontent.com/pod-product-compliance
Lightning Source LLC
Chambersburg PA
CBHW050651160426
43194CB00010B/1903